A Robbie Reader

DEBBY RYAN

Tammy Gagne

Mitchell Lane
PUBLISHERS

P.O. Box 196
Hockessin, Delaware 19707
Visit us on the web: www.mitchelllane.com
Comments? Email us: mitchelllane@mitchelllane.com

Mitchell Lane
PUBLISHERS

Printing   1   2   3   4   5   6   7   8   9

A Robbie Reader Biography

Aaron Rodgers	Drake Bell & Josh Peck	LeBron James
Abigail Breslin	Dr. Seuss	Mia Hamm
Adrian Peterson	Dwayne "The Rock" Johnson	Michael Strahan
Albert Einstein	Dwyane Wade	Miley Cyrus
Albert Pujols	Dylan & Cole Sprouse	Miranda Cosgrove
Alex Rodriguez	Eli Manning	Philo Farnsworth
Aly and AJ	Emily Osment	Raven-Symoné
Amanda Bynes	Emma Watson	Roy Halladay
AnnaSophia Robb	Hilary Duff	Selena Gomez
Ashley Tisdale	Jaden Smith	Shaquille O'Neal
Brenda Song	Jamie Lynn Spears	Story of Harley-Davidson
Brittany Murphy	Jennette McCurdy	Sue Bird
Carmelo Anthony	Jeremy Lin	Syd Hoff
Charles Schulz	Jesse McCartney	Taylor Lautner
Chris Johnson	Jimmie Johnson	Tiki Barber
Cliff Lee	Johnny Gruelle	Tim Lincecum
Dakota Fanning	Jonas Brothers	Tom Brady
Dale Earnhardt Jr.	Jordin Sparks	Tony Hawk
David Archuleta	Justin Beiber	Troy Polamalu
Debby Ryan	Keke Palmer	Tyler Perry
Demi Lovato	Larry Fitzgerald	Victoria Justice
Donovan McNabb		

Library of Congress Cataloging-in-Publication Data
Gagne, Tammy.
Debby Ryan / by Tammy Gagne.
    p. cm. — (A Robbie reader)
Includes bibliographical references and index.
Includes filmography.
ISBN 978-1-61228-332-6 (library bound)
1. Ryan, Debby, 1993– — Juvenile literature. 2. Actors — United States — Biography — Juvenile literature. 3. Singers — United States — Biography — Juvenile literature. I. Title.
PN2285.R94G35 2012
792.02'8092 — dc23
[B]
                                                                    2012018306
eBook ISBN: 9781612284002

ABOUT THE AUTHOR: Tammy Gagne is the author of numerous books for both adults and children, including *What It's Like to Be America Ferrera, Day by Day with Beyoncé, We Visit Mexico, Ways to Help Chronically Ill Children,* and *How to Convince Your Parents You Can Care for A Pet Racing Pigeon* for Mitchell Lane Publishers. As an avid volunteer, one of her favorite pastimes is visiting schools to speak to kids about the writing process. She lives in northern New England with her husband, son, dogs, and parrots.

TABLE OF CONTENTS

Words in **bold** type can be found in the glossary.

Debbie Ryan is known for her sweet tooth. Here she is enjoying a birthday treat at the Sugar Factory American Brassiere in Las Vegas, Nevada.

Three Cheers for Debby Ryan!

Debby Ryan has been on the move for as long as she can remember. She was born in Huntsville, Alabama on May 13, 1993. Soon thereafter, her family moved to Texas, where they stayed for five years. Her father was in the **military**, so they traveled around a lot. Their next move took them all the way to Germany.

Debby's father had been a huge fan of the Dallas Cowboys football team during their time in Texas. When he would watch the games, Debby would watch them too. What interested her the most, though, were the cheerleaders. As she told *American Cheerleader* magazine, "I loved the **uniformity** of it all and how glamorous it was, like when the lights hit their faces."

Debby brought this passion with her to Europe. Many cheerleaders start out by taking gymnastics, and Debby had already participated in gymnastics when she lived in Texas. In Germany, she and her family decided to start their own homeschool cheerleading league. Debby was just seven years old at the time.

The Ryans moved back to Forth Worth, Texas three years later. Debby was hoping to join Fossil Hill Middle School's cheerleading squad at this time, but she missed the deadline. Instead of dwelling on the missed opportunity, Debby immediately grabbed hold of another. She was offered the job of team **mascot**, and she took it. "I absolutely loved it!" she shares with *American Cheerleader.* "I hung out with the cheerleaders, and my best friend was even on the team while I was the mascot."

The outfit she had to wear had seen better days. By the time Debby took over the job, the old wildcat costume was falling apart. "I'd have to hot-glue the face back on every three weeks," she says. "It was bad." She also got teased for performing her mascot duties, but

The Suite Life on Deck stars Debby Ryan, Brittany Curran, and Kara Crane celebrate Brittany's birthday with friend, Anna Maria Perez of *Camp Rock*.

she took this in stride. She confided to *Girls' Life* magazine, "People made fun of me, but I have the best memories!" She still keeps that old costume in her dressing room today. Debby says it reminds her every day to bring a lot of energy to her performances.

One of Debby's first acting jobs was a small part in the 2008 film *The Longshots*. Debby's character, Edith, was the sidekick of the mean girl at school.

Her Big Break

Cheerleading wasn't the only activity Debby started in Europe. She also discovered acting there. When the family moved back to Texas in 2003, Debby asked her parents if she could start trying out for real acting jobs. Neither she nor they ever imagined that her career would take off as quickly as it did. Debby's original plan was to become a doctor. She explained to *American Cheerleader,* "I told my parents that I'd put the money I earned from acting towards med school, which was the only reason my dad said yes."

Debby's first professional acting jobs were small ones. Among them was a commercial for the foot-tapping, head-bobbing iDog mp3 speaker. She also won **bit parts** in the 2007 direct-to-video movie *Barney: Let's Go to the Firehouse*, and the 2008 film *The Longshots*.

Auditioning for acting parts meant spending a lot of time in California. This time it was Debby's career that made the travel necessary. In 2008, Debby landed her big break. The Disney Channel offered her the part of Bailey Pickett on a spin-off of the wildly popular *The Suite Life of Zack and Cody*. Debby remembers wanting the role very badly, but trying not to think about it too much.

"I sent my tape in November and got a call back in March saying I was in the top three. Then they asked me if I wanted to fly to L.A. to read with the stars of the show, Dylan and Cole Sprouse. When I got there, I was terrified and enthralled," she tells *American Cheerleader.* "Three days later I got a phone call." They wanted to know if she could move to L.A. in six days to start working on *The Suite Life on Deck*.

Playing Bailey proved to be a discovery process for Debby. Both she and her character on the show were teenagers who had recently

Debby and her co-stars Dylan Sprouse, Brenda Song, Cole Sprouse, and Phill Lewis visit the Disney Store in New York City to promote *The Suite Life on Deck* in 2009.

moved away from home. She says she learned how important her family and friends are to her, and she got into the habit of writing home often.

Of course, Debby had fun with her co-stars. Cole and Dylan were known for being big pranksters on the set. Debbie told *People* magazine that she was probably the hardest person for the twins to scare. "Sometimes Cole will pop out and scream in my face, and I'll literally not flinch . . . I have an older brother," she explains. Enough said.

Debby is very close to her older brother, Chase. In 2009 they attended the Los Angeles premiere of *Jonas Brothers: 3D Concert Experience* together.

A Sweet Life, Indeed

In addition to working on *The Suite Life on Deck*, Debby has made two movies for the Disney Channel in recent years. In 2010, she starred as Abby Jensen in *16 Wishes*, the story of a teen who receives a box of magical candles for her 16th birthday. The flick was a huge success, with 5.6 million viewers tuning in for its premiere. It has since been shown in more than 30 countries worldwide.

Not only did Debby act in the movie, but she also sang its theme song, "A Wish Comes True Every Day." Her older brother, Chase, is a singer and songwriter who helped her get even more involved with the movie's soundtrack. With his assistance, she wrote and **produced** an original song called "Open Eyes" for the film.

Debby and Chase grew up around music. "When I was six and we couldn't afford anything," she recalls in *American Cheerleader*, "my mom would take the guitar out and sing to us as we were falling asleep." Music still plays a meaningful role in their lives. When Debby made her big move to California, her brother was heading off to college. Because they are so close, he knew that being apart was going to be tough. Debby told *Girls' Life*, "Chase wrote me this really heartfelt song called 'Saying Goodbye.' He can help me overcome anything."

One thing Debby doesn't seem to need any help with is making a movie a big hit. In 2012 she starred in another Disney Channel Original Movie, *Radio Rebel*. The film's main character, Tara Adams, is an extremely shy high school student by day who secretly hosts a popular **podcast** each evening. The movie's premiere drew 4.3 million viewers.

Debby has quickly become one of Disney's most popular young stars. "I'm not completely submersed in Hollywood, though," she pointed out to *American Cheerleader.* "I keep myself and my loved ones a bit separated and

protected from it. It seems so glamorous until you're close to it." At the same time, she says that dressing up and walking the red carpet in front of screaming fans can be fun.

She also admits that she was a little star-struck when she met Brenda Song. "She is one of my favorite actresses!" Debby told *People.* "I just found a journal from when I was in fifth or sixth grade, and I wrote, 'If I could be best friends with a celebrity, it would be Brenda Song.'"

Debby poses with her *Jessie* co-stars Kevin Chamberlin, Skai Jackson, Cameron Boyce, Peyton List, and Karan Brar.

Introducing Jessie

When *The Suite Life on Deck* came to an end in 2011, it was a bittersweet experience for Debby. She told Cambio.com, "It was ultra dramatic. There was crying and pretending that we weren't crying. Laughing about the fact that we were crying. It was just a whole mess of emotions."

Debbie didn't waste any time between jobs. Her new Disney series *Jessie* premiered in 2011, and it is still going strong. The show is about a girl who comes to New York and unexpectedly becomes a nanny for a wealthy couple with numerous children. As Debby explained to *American Cheerleader*, "Three of their kids are adopted, so there are four different **cultures** and lifestyles all under one

Debby is seen here with Jake and Captain Hook from Disney's *Jake and the Never Land Pirates* at the 2012-2013 Disney Channel Worldwide Kids Upfront at the Hard Rock Cafe in New York City.

roof. The family has a private helicopter and a butler; they have the world literally at their fingertips."

Clearly, Debby is excited about her new show. She has even changed her looks to match her new role as Jessie Prescott. Debby's once blondish brown hair is now a deep auburn. She told *American Cheerleader*, "I want all of my characters to look a little bit different. So with *Jessie*, I really wanted to go red. I'm definitely bolder now, and my horizons are broader—I'm okay with being a little unpolished. I accept myself as I am, and you can too, if you want. If not, that's cool, too."

Of her two major television roles, Debby told Cambio.com she is more like Jessie. "I moved around a lot growing up, and I have an older brother. I'm tough. Bailey is pretty tough herself, but I moved around a lot and saw the world before I was like 10, and I feel like when you do that and you live that kind of life, you're captivated by the beauty in everyday things, whereas Bailey had visions of splendor. Yeah, I'm more like Jessie."

Debby strikes a rock star pose at Variety's 3rd Annual "Power of Youth" event with Taylor Spreitler of ABC Family's *Melissa & Joey*.

When She's Not Working . . .

Being an actress and singer are just two sides to Debby Ryan. In her spare time, she enjoys other activities. "I love reading," she told *People.* Like many young people, she sometimes has a hard time understanding Shakespeare, but this doesn't stop her from trying. "I'm working on *A Midsummer Night's Dream.* It's a soap opera, and it's even hard to understand in plain English." She says she carries the CliffsNotes study guide in her purse.

Even though she finds his work to be a bit challenging at times, Debby tells *Girls' Life* that she is smitten with Shakespeare's writing. "He could describe a junkyard and make it sound so beautiful, you'd want to hold your wedding there."

Debby brought her dog Presley to the Los Angeles premiere of her Disney Channel movie *16 Wishes* in 2010.

When Debby lived in Europe, she picked up the German language very quickly. "I used to be fluent . . ." she told *People.* "I have an ear for it." But coming back to the United States, she had a hard time readjusting to writing in English. Germans capitalize nouns, and when she returned to U.S., she wanted to do the same thing here. She said she just couldn't understand why the word "dog" was not capitalized in this country.

Debby also loves to get involved in charity work for a good cause. One of the causes she supports is Disney's Friends for Change. In 2011, Debby was one of more than 30 Disney stars who competed in the Disney Friends for Change Games. The stars were divided into groups that raised money for different environmental charities. Debby was captain of the Ocean Conservancy team. Ocean Conservancy works to protect the oceans of the world from overfishing, pollution, and the warming of the Arctic.

When she describes herself, Debby uses words like "nerd" and "dork." She says that not only was she in the chess club, but that she

Debby appears with *iCarly* star Nathan Kress at the Camp Ronald McDonald For Good Times 17th Annual Carnival at Universal Studios in Hollywood, California.

Debby attends an improv class at Bang Comedy Theatre with children from LA's BEST After School Enrichment Program in Los Angeles.

Debby spends her holiday at the Los Angeles Mission & Anne Douglas Center's Thanksgiving Meal for the Homeless.

also counted down the days until the next meeting. She confessed to *American Cheerleader*, "I trip over everything. I get caught in my headphones—I'm that kind of person. Things just happen around me; now I wear flat shoes to be safe."

Debby is obviously very comfortable with herself, and she hopes that any new opportunities that come her way give her a chance to express her uniqueness. "I want to do things that will make people say, 'That's interesting. I've never seen that before.' I'm just

Debby appears with Santa Paws at Walt Disney World's Magic Kingdom in Buena Vista, Florida. The Disney Parks Christmas Day Parade airs every year on ABC.

Few people can say that they have danced with First Lady Michelle Obama. Even fewer can say they did so along with Perry the Platypus from the Disney Channel cartoon *Phineas and Ferb*—but Debby can. All three were showing off their moves to celebrate the second anniversary of the "Let's Move" program to fight childhood obesity.

being me, and doing not only what I think would be best for my career, but what's best for me. You're only 18 once, and if you have opportunities, why would you pass them up?"

CHRONOLOGY

1993 Debby is born in Huntsville, Alabama on May 13.

2000 She and her family start a homeschool cheerleading league in Germany.

2003 The Ryans move back to the United States, settling in Fort Worth, Texas. Once there, Debby begins pursuing a career in acting.

2007 Wins a small role in *Barney: Let's Go to the Firehouse*.

2008 Is cast in a television commercial for the iDog mp3 speaker. Debby also appears in the movie *The Longshots* and lands a role on *The Suite Life on Deck*.

2010 Stars in the Disney Original Movie *16 Wishes*. She also performs an original song on the movie's soundtrack.

2011 Participates in the Disney Friends for Change Games as captain of the Ocean Conservancy team.

2012 Stars in the Disney Original Movie, *Radio Rebel*.

FILMOGRAPHY

2007	*Barney: Let's Go to the Firehouse*
2008	*The Longshots*
2010	*16 Wishes*
	What If . . .
2011	*The Suite Life Movie*
2012	*Radio Rebel*

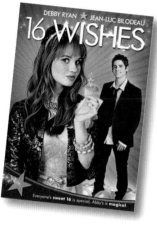

TELEVISION

2006	*Barney & Friends*
2008	*Yay Me! Starring London Tipton*
2009	*Wizards of Waverly Place*
	Hannah Montana
2008-2011	*The Suite Life on Deck*
2011	*Private Practice*
	R.L. Stine's The Haunting Hour
2012	*The Glades*
	So Random!
	Zeke and Luther
2011-present	*Jessie*

FIND OUT MORE

Books and Articles

Brooks, Riley. *Debby Ryan: Her Sweet Life.* New York: Scholastic, 2010.

Conrad, Kate. "Twelve Things About Debby Ryan." AOL Kids, January 13, 2011. http://kids.aol.com/2011/01/13/ twelve-things-about-debby-ryan/

Works Consulted

"Exclusive Interview: Debby Ryan Says 'Suite Life' Finale Was Bittersweet." Cambio.com, May 5, 2011. http://www.cambio.com/news/exclusive-interview- debby-ryan-says-suite-life-finale-was-bittersweet/#

Geragotelis, Brittany. "Debby Ryan: Disney's New It-Girl." *American Cheerleader*, October 2011.

"Girl Power," *People*, May 2009.

IMDb : Debby Ryan http://www.imdb.com/name/nm2913275/bio

Scarola, Danielle. "6 Things You Have to Know About Debby Ryan." *Girls' Life*, June/July 2010.

On the Internet

16 Wishes, The Movie http://16wishesthemovie.com/about-16-wishes/

Debby Ryan: Official Web Site http://www.debbyryan.com/

Who is Radio Rebel? http://www.whoisradiorebel.com/

WhoSay http://www.whosay.com/debbyryan

GLOSSARY

audition (aw-DISH-uhn)–A chance for an actor or other performer to try out for a part in a show or film.

bit part (bit PARHT)–A small speaking role in a movie, television show, or theater production.

culture (KULH-cher)–A set of beliefs and practices shared by people of a particular geographic area or ethnicity.

mascot (MAS-kot)–An animal or character that represents a team or other group, often believed to bring good luck.

military (MIL-i-ter-ee)–The armed forces who defend a country.

podcast (POD-kast)–An audio or video broadcast that can be accessed via the internet.

produce (pruh-DOOS)–To help create a movie or television show by paying for and overseeing all the technical aspects of it.

uniformity (yoo-nuh-FOR-mi-tee)–The quality of being the same.

INDEX